PIERRE AUGUSTE RENOIR

RENOIR

Robert F. Reiff
Professor of the History of Art
Middlebury College

McGRAW-HILL BOOK COMPANY · NEW YORK · LONDON · TORONTO · SYDNEY

Cover picture, *Dance in the Country* (1883), preliminary sketch, crayon, Private Collection. Photographs for Figures 1, 7, 9, and 10, courtesy Giraudon. Photograph for Figure 3, courtesy M. Knoedler & Co. Photograph for Figure 15, courtesy Durand-Ruel.

RENOIR'S WORK evokes a host of generally enchanting images: graceful, cultivated but unpretentious young women; naturally charming young children; splendid nudes enveloped in warm light and engaged in wholesome and totally innocent activity; shimmering scenes of rustic life; modest, accommodating views made glorious through heightened color and light. For Renoir painting was a kind of love affair, to be approached and developed less by rules or imitation than by instinct, and his total output would suggest that he instinctively chose subjects with broad popular appeal.

Renoir wanted his art to be characteristically French, enduring in significance, and yet vital to his own time. His approach is hedonistic and charged with a healthy optimism, but is never self-indulgent. His reverence for the grand traditions supersedes personal involvement and his works exhilarate, affirm, and cheer. His figures, particularly his nudes, lack the athletic animality of those of Degas, the palpable fullness of Courbet's, the monumentality of a Michelangelo nude, or the eroticism of an Ingres odalisque. Compared to them, Renoir seems uncomplicated. His genius lies in the fact that he offers the commonplace without sentimentality or mawkishness.

Renoir was born in 1841, the same winter as Claude Monet. Though Monet lived longer, Renoir had a full life, dying at the age of seventy-eight. They both lived to see the development of Cubism and the art of the Fauves by a new generation of young revolutionaries who dismissed the work of the Impressionists as not only tame, but decadent. Monet was accused of using sweetish, candy-box colors in his *Waterlilies* series. Renoir was revered as a patriarch, but largely by those close to his own generation. And yet, when Impressionism first came to the attention of the public it aroused a storm of protest such as no art movement has since.

It is generally true that artists do not begin their careers planning to be revolutionaries. Usually they have something they feel must be communicated, and that something turns

Frontispiece.
Self-Portrait
(1897), oil on canvas
16¼" x 13¼"
Sterling and Francine Clark
Art Institute, Williamstown
Massachusetts

[Facing this page]
Detail of Figure 12

5

out to be significantly radical. In retrospect the intentions of the Impressionists seem harmless, free of guile, modest, and sensible. Mostly they wanted to paint what they saw without any affectations, to disentangle themselves from hollow convention and reliance on formulae. This is not to say, of course, that Impressionist artists did not possess individual attitudes and special bias. Claude Monet, for example, by temperament rather than program, was the most committed, the true insurgent, the "pacemaker" of Impressionism as Lionello Venturi so aptly dubbed him.

Monet's vision was essentially empirical, as is revealed in some advice he gave an American woman painter: "When you go out to paint, try to forget what objects you have before you, a house, a field, or whatever. Merely think, here is a little square of blue, here an oblong of pink, here a streak of yellow, and paint it just as it looks to you, the exact color and shape, until it gives your own naive impression of the scene before you." When Monet recommended that the American forget what objects she had before her, he dispensed with a host of old conceptions about art: for instance, that it should instruct, uplift, reveal, and describe. When he said that objects should be reduced or abstracted to patches, dabs, streaks, and oblongs, he struck at traditional views on the rendering of form and on drawing.

Renoir was fully sympathetic to Monet's ideas, but when asked to expound his theories on art, he would become visibly irritated and dismiss the puzzled questioner. "Theories don't make good pictures," he is reported to have said. "For the most part they serve only to mask the shortcomings of the artist," and he added, "Theories are worked out afterwards in any case." Like any man he had opinions, but he voiced them in his work. His painting reveals he believed above all that life was meant to be enjoyed. He approved of a life that was simple, direct, and natural—having friends, some comforts, a loving wife and family, and doing something one liked to do and doing it well.

In Renoir's time there were many intellectuals who had long abandoned the idea that the material progress promised by industrial advances could be equated with a new golden age. They not only rejected their own time but felt a need to start all over again. They reasoned that the ancient past and the peoples from distant, "primitive" lands would yield an answer because they were unburdened by civilization and, therefore, close to nature and the source of true creativity. Such thinking led Gauguin to leave his home and family and to strike out for Tahiti. Renoir traveled to North Africa, although mainly as a tourist, but he too instinctively felt that an artist must rely not merely on accumulated knowledge or "culture," but on his own sensibilities and impulses. He took delight in simple pleasures and experienced warmth and security in binding human relationships. He did not paint the Alps, but rather the meadow full of poppies not far from his door. He glorified the world around him as a potential paradise. Unlike Zola, Renoir rejected the sordid. He was not a protester, and one cannot imagine the happy young group in his *Moulin de la Galette* (Slide 9) ever suffering or growing old. Renoir fixes in time the golden moments, moments that exist, but that cannot be sustained—except in art.

Pierre Auguste Renoir was born on February 25, 1841, in Limoges, a city famed for its ceramic and enamel work. He had three brothers and one sister. His father, a tailor, could barely support the large family in Limoges, so, in 1845, he took them to Paris where they settled for good; Renoir always considered himself a Parisian.

At an early age Renoir showed an aptitude for drawing, and his father decided to turn this natural gift to a useful end by apprenticing the boy at age thirteen to a painter of porcelain. He was soon doing piece work, being paid so much for a tiny bouquet of roses, more for a profile of Marie Antoinette and other more complicated motifs. Though content to continue in this field, Renoir was forced to leave when techniques were perfected to decorate china mechanically. At seventeen he found himself searching for a new career, and turned to painting decorations on fans, copying works by the seventeeth-century artists Watteau, Lancret, and Boucher.

This early experience as a commercial decorator had an enduring influence on Renoir's art. Throughout his career he favored lightly pigmented surfaces, transparent glazes, and even a palette of strawberry reds, moss greens, warm golds, and cobalts and lavenders, which may have derived from his porcelain-decorating experiences. Certainly the early copying of designs by Watteau and Boucher imbued him with an unending admiration for these Rococo masters with their soft palette and delight in sensual beauty. He told the art dealer Vollard that Boucher's *Diana at the Bath* (Figure 1) was not only his first love, but a life-time infatuation. As a young man he frequently had visited the Louvre, often during his lunch hour, and spent many hours there drawing from the antique which he also loved and which later influenced his art.

By 1862 Renoir had saved enough from his meager earnings to study at the École des Beaux-Arts and with the Swiss academician Charles Gleyre (1808–1874), a rather uninspiring teacher whose chief merit, Renoir later explained, was that he left his students to their own devices. The young artist was considered promising enough to be given free tuition for a few additional courses. His teachers tried to discourage his natural affinity for color by warning that, following such a path, he might become another Delacroix—an "insult" that must have delighted Renoir, for he loved Delacroix's bold use of color. "While I was at Gleyre's, the Louvre for me meant Delacroix," he once told his son. Several of his fellow students, Sisley, Bazille, and particularly Claude Monet, were openly in revolt against Gleyre and the dry, academic style he represented. Their sympathies were with progressive artists who appeared as free, inquiring spirits because their views ran strictly counter to those of the École academicians. Corot, Courbet, Jongkind, Boudin, and Diaz were their heroes. Renoir and his friends were receptive to their new ideas of naturalistic color and subject. Renoir, for instance, gave up the use of black to darken tones in his earliest paintings after the Barbizon painter Diaz, whom he had met in the forest of Fontainebleau, chided him for his dark palette and explained that "even the shadows of the leaves have light in them."

Renoir's meeting with Diaz did much to open the eyes of the young man and led to a sense of expanding horizons and to new revelations. He had discovered Delacroix and Courbet and Manet (whose *Déjeuner sur l'Herbe* was exhibited at the Salon des Refusés in 1863), and

Figure 1.
François Boucher (1703-1770)
Diana at Her Bath
(1742), oil on canvas
22½" x 28¾"
Louvre, Paris

his art reflects the influence of these modern masters as well as that of his fellow student and companion Monet. Although Renoir settled into no single style and favored no one group of themes, all of his work bears the indisputable stamp of his own personality.

Renoir could have been a successful academician. In 1863 he had a painting entitled *Esmeralda* accepted by the jury for the annual Salon, where academic art and that which was thought to adhere to academic standards was exhibited. More than an honor, acceptance for the Salon was almost essential for success and financial security. A painting stamped on the back with an "R," for rejection, was not apt to find a ready buyer. Renoir nevertheless destroyed his *Esmeralda,* partly because he found it cumbersome to store, partly and largely because he had used as a darkening agent the unstable pigment bitumen, a coal tar which gives glossy, slick blacks when fresh but turns grayish and mottled with time.

Renoir continued to send works to the Salon, which were accepted or rejected depending on the liberality of the jury, although he usually chose to send his least "revolutionary" works. He had works accepted in 1865, 1868, 1869, and 1870, and rejected in 1866, 1867, and 1872. It wasn't until 1878 that he again submitted a work to the jury. The following year he showed his *Portrait of Madame Charpentier and Her Children* (Slide 10) at the Salon, and for the first time he enjoyed a great popular success. The lure of official recognition did not abate, and Renoir exhibited in the Salon several times before 1890, when he was last represented. Renoir, like Manet and Degas, respected tradition. Manet, whose art relates particularly to that of Hals and Velásquez, learned principally by going to the great museums of Europe. Degas claimed Ingres as a major influence in his artistic life. Renoir, however, could be quite irreverent about certain old masters. He found Michelangelo and Bernini tiring, and said of Leonardo, "He bores me. He ought to have stuck to his flying machines." What the Impressionists deplored was not tradition, but the state to which contemporary official art had deteriorated. By the late 1850s the Salon had become little more than a bazaar for paintings. Most of the work was directed to the naive patron, whose tastes went toward the anecdotal, sentimental, and highly finished and detailed. The French government would select large esthetic works whose "noble" themes, generally historical or classical, were formula-ridden and full of empty rhetoric.

Monet and Degas in particular, and Renoir, Sisley, Pissarro, Bazille, Guillaumin, and Berthe Morisot had developed their own various expressions of Impressionism before the movement was given its name. In fact, the beginnings of Impressionism can be traced back to the first quarter of the nineteenth century to Constable and Corot. Elements of Impressionist styles appear in the work of the Romantics, in Courbet, in the landscapes of the Barbizon painters, Theodore Rousseau, Daubigny, Diaz, and in Jongkind and Boudin, the mentors of Monet. Of course, "impressionistic" painting per se is as old as art itself. Any painting which stresses natural light at the expense of sharply defined images and narrative detail can be said to be "impressionist." There are Pompeian and Sung-dynasty paintings which are called impressionist. Vermeer is frequently called an impressionist, and Watteau too. Thus, basic tenets of the Impressionist movement, such as loose brushwork and interest in effects of momentary light, far from being the malicious invention of a few misguided artists as many of Renoir's contemporaries were inclined to think, actually can be found in many other periods in the history of art.

Monet and Degas represent the two extremes of nineteenth-century Impressionism, Monet concentrating on fleeting effects of light as seen out-of-doors and Degas on the momentary pose of the performing figure caught unawares, often under artificial light. Monet set up his easel in the fields and depended entirely on his eye for the conception of his painting, whereas Degas didn't believe in painting *en plein air* and is recorded as having said that the air we breathe is not that found in Old-Master paintings. Degas also said, "No art is as little spontaneous as mine. What I do is the result of reflection and the study of the great masters." But at the same time he sought the look of spontaneity and casually caught movement and slaved to acquire it. Like Monet he used broken color freely and imaginatively, and many of his paintings are essentially elevated sketches. Renoir had a high opinion of Degas, whom he considered a great sculptor, but was never influenced by him.

Though Renoir was much closer to and greatly influenced by his friend Monet, he was not committed to any program or style. His *Pont des Arts, Paris,* dated 1868, shows sharp and neatly defined forms, while the lovely *La Grenouillère* (Slide 4), done the same year, seems almost to be the work of another hand. *Diana* and *Lise* (Slides 2 and 3), both of the previous year, are also quite different, with the former stressing pattern and the latter Courbet-like bulk (Figure 2). Some of Renoir's loveliest works of this early, formative period are his flower-pieces. Despite its unevenness, his art of the late sixties and early seventies is wonderfully fresh; it communicates the excitement and intoxication of a young man making discoveries.

Renoir and his friends worked during the day and at night would frequent a café to enjoy each other's company and discuss art. From 1866 the Café Guerbois was favored. Edouard Manet had discovered it and, as the articulate elder spokesman for a new artistic movement, in a sense held court there. He attracted friends and admirers who in turn brought with them interested intellectuals. Zola, Duranty, Astruc, Duret, and Bazille attended these sessions. Renoir, Degas, Monet, Pissarro, Sisley, Fantin-Latour, and Cézanne would drop in whenever they were in Paris. It was a lively place, as Monet later recalled: "Nothing could be more interesting than these causeries with their perpetual clash of opinions. They kept our wits sharpened, they encouraged us with stories of enthusiasm that for weeks and weeks kept us up, until the final shaping of the idea was accomplished. From them we emerged tempered more highly, with a firmer will, with our thoughts clear and more distinct." Renoir rarely took part in discussion since he considered theorizing about art pointless and unnatural. "A swallow speeds through the air to catch a gnat and to satisfy its hunger, not to verify a principle," he was quoted as saying. He even disliked being called an "artist," considering it pretentious. Instead, he thought of himself as a "workman-painter," a kind of elevated artisan, but not an intellectual. Renoir felt quite strongly in this respect. In fact, he went so far as to call the brain "an ugly thing." He maintained that he didn't like the company of men

Figure 2.
Gustave Courbet (1819-1877)
Bather Sleeping by a Brook
(1845), oil on canvas
32″ x 25½″
Detroit Institute of Arts

because they were "too tense" and thought too much. As an artist, he felt he was little more than a skilled agent capable of receiving images and then transmitting them through some medium such as paint, crayon, or clay.

During the Franco-Prussian War of 1870 the solidarity of the group was temporarily disrupted. Sisley, a British subject, Monet, and Pissarro fled to England. Manet and Degas, on the other hand, thought it their responsibility as gentlemen and aristocrats to take up arms against the foe and enlisted. Bazille joined a regiment of Zouaves and died in combat a few months later. Renoir was called into service and placed in a light cavalry regiment far from the front. He was not only unharmed, but had a rather pleasurable, easy time and was commissioned to paint portraits of his company commander and his wife. Once the peace had been settled, Renoir and the others began to trickle back to Paris to renew old ties and to paint.

In the five years that followed, Renoir seemed to show no more disposition to develop a consistent style than he had prior to the war. One of his first paintings, the *Odalisque* (Slide 5), is decidedly in the manner of Delacroix. Two years later he returned to a similar theme with his *Parisian Women Dressed as Algerians*. His fondness for Rubens is expressed in certain of his portraits and figure studies. He used a light impasto and translucent glazes as did Rubens and even gave to his women some of the quality seen, for instance, in Rubens' lovely *Le Chapeau de Paille* in London. Renoir would frequently paint the costume and setting with long brush strokes in a free and sketchy manner, whereas he would refine his treatment for the head and hands. He employed different methods of applying paint in the landscapes as well.

These differences, as mentioned previously, are evident in two works done in 1868, his *Pont des Arts* and his *La Grenouillère* (Slide 4). The former suggests Monet's influence, and Renoir was to continue in this manner in his 1872 *Pont Neuf* (Figure 3), though not with the same deliberateness. In *La Grenouillère,* a scene painted also by Monet (Figure 4), he fused tones, causing one to merge with the other in a fabric of shifting color areas, each with subtle variations of texture. In this work objects are not defined as much as they are solicited into being. Degas remarked once that Renoir played with color the way a kitten does with a ball of yarn. The manner seen in *La Grenouillère* was the one he would develop and maintain in later landscapes. These have a homogeniety of style not seen in his portraits or his nudes.

Inconsistencies in Renoir's style may be interpreted as an expression of his easy attitude and temperament. "I am like a little cork thrown on the water and carried by the current," he was reported as saying. "In painting, I simply let myself go." In life, too, he believed in adjusting to situations and did not make a consistently concerted effort to channel energies and impulses toward any specified end. And yet the years from about 1870 to 1883 can be considered Renoir's Impressionist period and the heyday of that movement. It was during the first half of this time span that Renoir and his friends were consolidated as a group with the single aim of achieving broader recognition.

Figure 3.
Le Pont Neuf
(1872), oil on canvas
29¼″ x 36½″
Private Collection, New York

Figure 4.
Claude Monet (1840-1926)
La Grenouillère
oil on canvas, 29⅜″ x 39¼″
Metropolitan Museum of Art, New York
Bequest of Mrs. H. O. Havemeyer, 1929
The H. O. Havemeyer Collection

The Impressionists, young and unrecognized, had a few patrons but none so rich as to support the whole group, though Renoir acquired affiliation with the dealer Paul Durand-Ruel in 1873. Durand-Ruel had been farsighted enough to purchase works by members of the Barbizon School which brought high prices much later, and now also acquired paintings by the Impressionists and exhibited them in his galleries in London and Paris. But the prosperity of the postwar years was followed in late 1873 by a sudden depression that forced Durand-Ruel to abandon his support of the young nonconformists, at least for the time being. In desperation, the group decided that the time had come for them to arrange a show of their own, and on April 15, 1874, in the second-floor photography studio of their friend Nadar on the Boulevard des Capucines in the heart of Paris, their first group show opened.

Thirty artists in all exhibited in this event. It was indeed a mixed group. Eight of them—Cézanne, Degas, Boudin, Morisot, Monet, Pissarro, Sisley, and Renoir—have since been recognized as being among the century's and France's greatest artists. One hundred and sixty-five pictures were included. Renoir showed six, and since all were relatively conventional, critics were kindest to him. It was Cézanne they attacked mercilessly. Monet exhibited a work entitled *Impression-Sunrise* which seemed to one critic to epitomize what he deplored most of all, what seemed to be a perverse lack of concern for clarity and form; he claimed that it was at best nothing more than a sketch and Monet, a mere "impressionist."

The group had given themselves a rather cumbersome name, *Société anonyme des artistes, peintres, sculpteurs, graveurs, etc.,* whose sole virtue was accuracy. It was rather the abusive nickname given to them by the critic which caught on, and instead of spurning the epithet they adopted it and changed the name of their loose organization to *Peintres Impressionistes.* The exhibit was well-attended and was at least a *succès de scandale.* It won the group notoriety but not recognition, and certainly brought them no financial benefits, for not a single work was sold. An auction of their works the following year was an unqualified fiasco. However, Renoir did meet the remarkable customs employee Victor Chocquet, who despite his modest means not only purchased paintings, but later commissioned works. Renoir painted both Chocquet's portrait (Figure 5) and that of his wife.

Disheartening events caused moments of black despair for the artists. Claude Monet suffered most of all. Deeply in debt, months behind in his rent, he was forced to vacate his home, and he and his family hardly had enough to eat. Yet Monet sternly refused to take commissions, considering them a compromise. Renoir, however, had no such scruples and managed adequately with his portraits and nudes. However, none of the paintings of the Impressionists reflected their feelings of despondency at this time or any other. In fact, the paintings move in quite the opposite direction, full of sunshine, youthful buoyancy, and a lightness of touch.

Nearly a hundred years have passed since the first truly Impressionist paintings were executed. When they first appeared, and for a period of about fifteen years, they were generally rejected. It is difficult to understand why these pleasant, sun-filled landscapes, these views of vacationers in their sailboats, of city folk paddling about in the water or picnicking, could

have caused so much resentment. Actually, it was not the bright color or the thematic material which upset the gallery visitors so much as the rendering. The works looked as unfinished as sketches for detailed, fully conceived versions, and the critics thought it an affront to put a frame around a rapidly brushed-in piece and then pass it off as art.

Although the Impressionists painted in different ways and, as has been pointed out, had no expressed program, their painting still had certain broad characteristics in common. In general, Impressionists painted what they saw, not qualities they knew to exist. When we look at a scene through a window, we have no first-hand, immediate awareness of temperature, of tactile values and weight, or of the total dimensions of the objects before us. We know that a distant tree looks pretty much the same from the opposite side, that its bark is not as cool and smooth as glass, and that swinging a fist against the trunk will reveal its considerable hardness. But we know this from *a priori* experience, not from what the eye reveals, for all it sees is areas, colors, and tones. If one views a scene through a coarse screen, all one sees is spots of color, not forms. Impressionists, of course, were not merely "eyes." Even Monet, the most orthodox of the Impressionists, creates the effect of a heightened, energized vision. His colors are a bit brighter than normally experienced, his forms are abstracted to spots for greater visual impact, and he delights us with the way he can evoke a sea breeze or the sparkle of gentle waves on the Seine with the touch and weight of his brush. Even so, it is this kind of empirical, molecular vision which makes Impressionist art distinctive.

It can be said that the Impressionist tends to look at the world in a somewhat detached manner, that he assumes the role of a receptive, aloof, and contemplative spectator whose attitude is objective but also aesthetic. The Impressionist displays little or no interest in the political, heroic, fantastic, idealistic, literary, humanitarian, or sentimental; his chief aim is to communicate the visible and the transitory.

Impressionist paintings are immediately recognizable. Most obvious are the bright, "rainbow" colors and the way they are allowed to mix in the eye. Blues and violets replace browns and grays. Glossy finished surfaces are replaced by a textural quality with brushstrokes seen separately from one another and evidencing the degree of pressure exerted. Forms are translated into purely painterly terms as strokes, patches, lines, and pattern. There are no precisely stated hierarchies of importance as may be seen, for example, in a Renaissance Adoration, where one is guided along converging lines to the significant center of attention. Rather, there is a trend toward randomness, even in the composition. Finally, subject matter, drawn almost exclusively from the contemporary scene, tends to lack extra-aesthetic values. When Monet painted Rouen Cathedral, it was not as a religious structure but as a coruscated screen absorbing and reflecting light. In general, Impressionist pictures are small, which is understandable when one realizes they were painted for the most part out-of-doors, and the canvas had to be portable.

Renoir painted his finest, happiest, most vibrant works between 1874, with the superb *La Loge,* and 1881, with his *Luncheon of the Boating Party* (Slide 7 and Figure 6). Falling within this span are *The Swing, Moulin de la Galette* (Slide 9), *The First Outing, The Boat-*

Figure 5.
Portrait of Victor Chocquet
(1876), oil on canvas
18″ x 14″
Collection Oskar Reinhart
Winterthur, Switzerland

Figure 6.
The Luncheon of the Boating Party
(1881), oil on canvas
51" x 68"
Phillips Collection, Washington, D.C.

ing Party at Chatou, The Rowers' Lunch (Slide 13), *The Cup of Chocolate,* and some superb portraits of his friends Monet (Figure 7), Sisley and his wife (Figure 8), Cézanne, and his patrons Chocquet and Madame Charpentier, as well as several landscapes and views of sail-boats on the Seine. Within this period of about ten years he created the masterpieces which establish his reputation as a great artist. Works prior to and following this decade rarely rise to the heights realized by his *Moulin de la Galette* or *Luncheon of the Boating Party,* in which Renoir fully realized his powers as an artist. He was no longer searching for direction, but the excitement of discovery continued, transformed into a freshness, savor, and spirited innovation. He acted with the confidence of an independent, accomplished, vitally youthful yet mature man, who knows what he wants and strives toward it without qualms or self-doubt.

In 1871 Monet settled in Argenteuil, a small, pretty town on the Seine not far from Paris, where he could live less expensively than in the French capital. Renoir, Manet, Caillebotte, Sisley, Bertha Morisot, and Pissarro frequented the area. No other site has been more closely identified with Impressionism than Argenteuil. Edouard Manet was so enchanted by the place and by the new manner of painting that he lightened his palette and, in his own peculiar way, became an Impressionist too. As they had done earlier, in 1868 at La Grenouillère, Monet and Renoir worked side-by-side. In 1874 Renoir painted *Sailboats in Argenteuil* (Slide 6), as did Monet (Figure 9). While not identical, these two paintings are strikingly similar in conception.

Renoir was to spend most of his summers in the country at such places as Berneval on the Channel coast in 1879; at Croissy, an island in the Seine, the following year; and at nearby Wargemont in 1881. That same year he visited Algeria in the spring, and in the fall he and Aline Charigot married and honeymooned in Italy, traveling through Venice, Florence, Rome, Naples, Capri, and Pompeii. Renoir loved Venice and painted a number of characteristic scenes of gondolas on the canals and of such landmarks as San Marco (Slide 14). He was enthusiastic about the frescoes in Pompeii because of their unaffectedness and because there was "no genius, no soul-searching." While in Palermo, he met Wagner and made an oil sketch of him. Since Renoir had longed for many years to see the treasures in the museums abroad, particularly in Italy, the journey became something of a pilgrimage.

The highlight of Renoir's trip came when he saw the frescoes of Raphael in the Vatican. He was overwhelmed by their rich complexity, their breadth, and the controlled definition of the forms. For some time Renoir had harbored severe doubts concerning the limitations of Impressionism with its stress on the effects of light at the expense of other values, and the sight of the monuments in Rome convinced him all the more that he had veered too far from the traditional path and that some program of reform was necessary. Though he had rejected the empty artifices of the academy, he never lost his respect for tradition. He had expressed a growing critical feeling toward Impressionism when he had declined to include works in the 1879, 1880, and 1881 Impressionist exhibitions; however, it was not his intention to abandon Impressionism, but to enrich his paintings with values of form, line, and volume, which he

Figure 7.
Portrait of Monet
(1875), oil on canvas
33¾″ x 24″
Louvre, Paris

Figure 8.
Sisley and his Wife
(1868), oil on canvas
41" x 29¼"
Wallraf-Richartz Museum
Cologne

Figure 9.
Claude Monet (1840-1926)
Sailboats at Argenteuil
(1875), oil on canvas
23½″ x 31½″
Louvre, Paris

thought had been neglected. As his art testifies, he retained contemporary subject matter, an Impressionist palette, and confidence in the primacy of instinct and sensibility as forces in the art of creation.

On his way home to Paris, Renoir stopped off at Marseilles and then went on to L'Estaque to renew his acquaintance with Cézanne. What was originally meant to be a short visit had to be extended to over two months when Renoir developed pneumonia. One finds it difficult to imagine Renoir being friends with Cézanne, who was humorless, deeply suspicious, and a mountain of obstinacy, and yet friends they were. Furthermore, Renoir appreciated Cézanne's abilities and called him the greatest artist to appear in France since the Romanesque period, a bold and courageous statement and one with which critics only recently could agree. He also claimed that Cézanne could apply only three patches of color to a canvas and that these would indeed be right. Renoir had extraordinary insight and sophistication for a man who valued unaffected simplicity and professed to believe that art was an act of spontaneous creation, as ingenuous as the blossoming of a flower.

Cézanne, like Renoir, believed in the classical tradition. Yet, while he admired Poussin and strove to emulate the French classicist, but within the context of Impressionist discovery, the austere, unbending Cézanne was not so much a classicist as a repressed Romantic, who sublimated his carnal passions to passion for constructive vision. Renoir's classicism, if indeed it can be called that, was the expression of an aesthetic conscience. For a while he considered himself wayward and in grave need of self-discipline for having neglected line at the expense of color. "About 1883, I had wrung Impressionism dry," Renoir recalled to Walter Pach, "and I finally came to the conclusion that I knew neither how to paint nor how to draw. In a word, Impressionism was a blind alley, as far as I was concerned." Then he noted, ". . . light plays too great a part outdoors; you have no time to work out the composition." Working directly from nature, Renoir concluded, leads the artist to be overly concerned with catching and fixing momentary effects at the expense of line, form, and interesting composition. Thus, in such a frame of mind, Renoir entered what art historians have variously called his "harsh," "dry," "sour" phase, his *periode aigre.*" To most critics, there was more loss than gain during this interval of self-reform. But Renoir was grimly determined in his efforts and went so far as to destroy a number of canvases which failed to measure up to his new standards. In 1883 he had come upon the fourteenth-century treatise on painting by Cennino Cennini and studied it carefully. Cennini gave advice to artists working in egg tempera since oil painting was used primarily in domestic decoration and even then not extensively. Egg tempera demands conciseness in defining form and requires that these forms be rigidly circumscribed by closed contours. A charge made by a critic that Renoir couldn't draw as well as Degas so obsessed him that he took to making many drawings in preparing a work. For example, he made a number of preparatory drawings, based directly on seventeenth-century bas-reliefs by Girardon, for his *Bathers,* sometimes called *Les Grandes Baigneuses* (see Figures 10 and 11 and Slide 16).

Figure 10.
François Girardon (1628-1715)
Bathing Nymphs (details)
(1668-70), bas-relief
Garden of Versailles

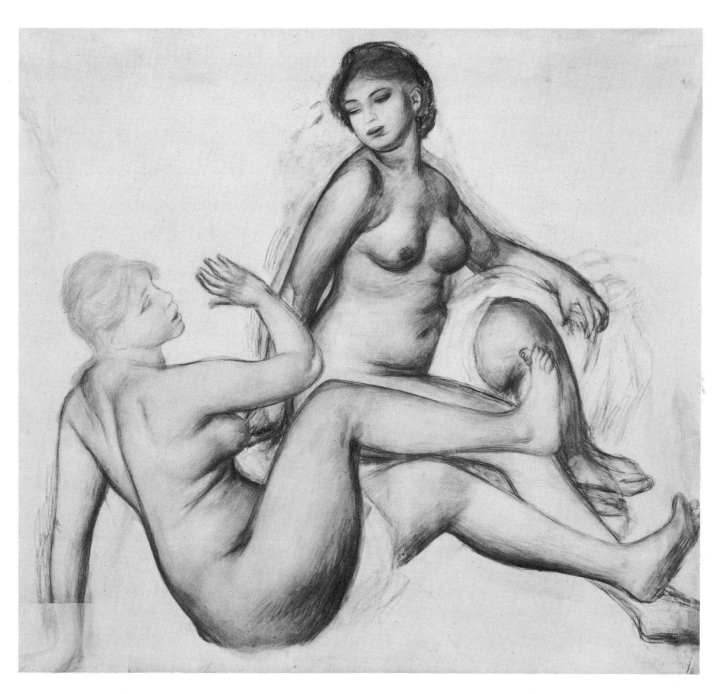

Figure 11.
The Bathers, (1883), drawing
49½″ x 55⅛″
Fogg Art Museum, Harvard
University, Cambridge, Massachusetts
Maurice Wertheim Collection

Even during this period Renoir reveals a certain ambivalence of style in his painting. For instance, in the *Dance at Bougival* (Figure 12) of 1883, he defines the central pair with a new concern for solidity of form, but the figures seated at the table recall those in his *Moulin de la Galette.* Renoir admitted in a letter to his dealer, Durand-Ruel, in 1884, "I have lost a great deal, working in the four square meters of the studio. I would have gained ten years had I followed Monet's example [to work out-of-doors] a little." He is much more consistent in his *Umbrellas,* also dated 1883, which has an undeniable monotony, but which has as well much of the old Renoir spirit and charm (Figure 13). However, one senses the greatest loss in his denial of rainbow color. Color resists method and organization, and as artists have known for centuries, color tends to suffer when form dominates. Despite his periodic doubts, Renoir continued to pursue his puritanical path, drawing all details, often every leaf on a tree, before he took up his brush to apply pigment. But about 1888 he began to relent, and later he swung to the other direction, painting in a most unfettered style toward the end of his career. Even so, one aspect of his "harsh" period continued: his choice of subject. He was to drift away from themes with a specific contemporary emphasis, as characterized in his 1866 *At the Inn of Mother Anthony* (Figure 14), and to concentrate on the female nude, a subject so universal as to belong to no time or place, one endowed with classical allusions. Although he did several portraits, many so informal in nature that they recall his work of the 1870s, it was the "classical" theme of the nude which predominated.

Renoir had never been a bohemian in the Gauguin tradition, nor, for that matter, had any of the other Impressionists. A family man by choice and temperament, he loved the comfort of his home and was devoted to his wife and his three children, Pierre, Jean (his biographer), and Claude, nicknamed "Coco." As he grew older his family became increasingly important to him. In fact, he depended on them completely for his care after 1912, when he was confined to a wheelchair with crippling arthritis. His first attack, in December, 1888, left his face partially paralyzed. But even when he was at his worst, there was no let-up in activity. He went to Spain in 1892 and spent summers at many of his favorite old haunts, Pont-Aven, Aix-en-Provence, and Louveciennes. In 1896 he went to Bayreuth to hear the Wagner *Ring Cycle,* and as late as 1910 he visited Munich. While he returned again and again to Aix-les-Bains to receive medical treatment, all this time he continued to paint. Although his hands became increasingly crippled, Renoir did a few large-scale works which reveal considerable control, such as *At the Piano* (1892) (Slide 17), *The Breakfast at Bernevel* (1898), and a *Judgment of Paris* (1910). He still accepted a few portrait commissions. His portrait of his biographer and dealer, Ambroise Vollard, dated 1908 and now in the Courtauld Institute Galleries, is one of the finest of his late works, as is his self-portrait executed in 1910 (Figure 15). Most of his late works are either nudes or female models, most often the young girls who worked around his house, such as Gabrielle. They are shown combing their hair, strumming on a mandolin, or holding the Renoir children. The landscapes of his later years are most freely executed and lack any reference to specific terrain. Some are so abstract as to be little more than lush orchestrations of iridescent color.

Figure 12.
Dance at Bougival
(1883), oil on canvas
70″ x 38″
Museum of Fine Arts, Boston

Figure 13.
Umbrellas
(1881)
oil on canvas
71″ x 45¼″
National Gallery
London

Figure 14.
*At the Inn
of Mother Anthony*
(1866)
oil on canvas
76½″ x 51½″
National Museum
Stockholm

Figure 15.
Self-Portrait
(1910), oil on canvas
16½″ x 12″
Private Collection

These late works depart a long way from the original intent of Impressionism; it is almost as if Renoir had stopped observing nature and had turned his full energies to his canvas. His palette becomes quite hot with crushed strawberry tones, golden siennas, corals, purples, and vermillions; this last period has been called his "red" period. The atmosphere is thick and moist as on a hot day after a rain in early summer. Figures loom large. Nudes become massive, inert, and unburdened by thought. These great, bovine beings overwhelm us with their sheer bulk, while at the same time they disarm us with their total innocence. Contours are muffled and distinctions between form and setting so obscured and relaxed as to suggest a sense of ease and well-being, bordering on lassitude.

Renoir, too impatient to discuss his painting or art in general when he was young, was less reluctant as an old man. In a most revealing interview with the American painter and writer Walter Pach in 1912, Renoir described his manner of working at that time:

> I arrange my subject as I want it, then I go ahead and paint it, like a child. I want a red to be sonorous, to sound like a bell; if it doesn't turn out that way, I add more reds and other colors until I get it. I am no cleverer than that. I have no rules and no methods; anyone can look at my materials or watch how I paint—he will see that I have no secrets. I look at a nude; there are myriads of tiny tints. I must find the ones that will make the flesh on my canvas live and quiver. Nowadays they want to explain everything. But if they could explain a picture, it wouldn't be art. Shall I tell you what I think are the two qualities of art? It must be indescribable and it must be inimitable. . . . The work of art must seize upon you, wrap you up in itself, carry you away. It is the means by which the artist conveys his passions; it is the current which he puts forth which sweeps you along in his passion.

In 1913, at Vollard's insistence, Renoir turned to sculpture. Previously he had only experimented with the medium. In 1907 he had executed a medallion and a bust of his youngest son, Coco (Figure 16), and these are the only works made entirely by Renoir. The others, such as *The Judgment of Paris* (Figure 17), are the product of a partnership with a young Italian sculptor, Richard Guino. The collaboration was remarkably successful. Renoir selected drawings and sections of paintings which the self-effacing Guino translated into sculpture while Renoir, seated in his wheelchair, directed the activity with a pointer.

In his absorbing book, *Renoir, My Father,* Jean Renoir recalls his father's physical state during his last years. "His emaciated face wore an expression of affectionate mockery . . . his hands were terribly deformed. His rheumatism had made the joints stiff and caused the thumbs to turn inward towards the palms, and his fingers to bend towards the wrists." However, even under these most torturous conditions, Renoir continued to paint up to his death. Jean Renoir has corrected the myth that the brush was strapped to his father's hand. "The truth is that his skin had become so tender that contact with the wooden handle of the brush injured it. . . . to avoid this difficulty he had a little piece of cloth inserted in the hollow of his hand. His twisted fingers gripped rather than held the brush."

Figure 16.
Head of Coco
(1908), bronze
10¾″ x 7½″
Knoedler Gallery, New York

Figure 17.
The Judgment of Paris
(1914) bronze, 29¼" x 35½" x 6¾"
Cleveland Museum of Art
Purchase from the J. H. Wade Fund
Executed by Richard Guino after
drawing by Renoir and under his direction

In 1915, Renoir lost his wife, and four years later on December 3, 1919, he died. During his last trip to Paris just before his death, he was invited to the Louvre as its sole visitor and was taken from room to room in his invalid's chair. While there he had the joy of viewing his own portrait of Mme. Charpentier, a study done in 1886 or 1887 preparatory to the large portrait of Mme. Charpentier and her children (Slides 10 and 11). Although Renoir suffered considerable physical discomfort in his old age, he must have received rare satisfaction from seeing his art so honored in his lifetime. He had already assumed a place alongside the great masters of the past.

1: PORTRAIT OF MADEMOISELLE ROMAINE LACAUX (1864)
oil on canvas, 32″ x 25⅛″
Cleveland Museum of Art, Gift of the Hanna Fund

This portrait is generally conceded to be the earliest signed and dated work by Renoir to come down to us. The artist destroyed much of his painting done prior to 1866, possibly because he disapproved of its general darkness of tone. If this early portrait is characteristic of those works now lost, there is reason to grieve, for this is an accomplished, appealing piece.

The Lacaux family were vacationing at Barbizon when they met the young Renoir and commissioned him to paint the portrait of their young daughter. Renoir had just finished his period of study with Gleyre, so this work must have been one of his first commissions, and he has obviously sought to please his patrons.

The young lady sits upright in a hard chair, with her gaze directed at the painter. The formality of the pose and the placement of a curtain in the background are reminiscent of the manner of Titian or one of the past masters. The color scheme of red, white, and blue is applied with such subtlety that the tricolor is never suggested, and the flesh tones are lustrous and as delicate as finely wrought china. The sitter rests her hands on red flowers, the same shade as the stones in her earrings. A bluish haze has reduced the shape of the flowers beyond the curtain to something akin to a palpitating screen, and this could be interpreted as symbolic of the future expectations of the youthful sitter on the verge of womanhood.

2: DIANA (1867), oil on canvas, 70¾″ x 50½″
National Gallery of Art, Washington, D.C., Chester Dale Collection

Renoir had hoped to conquer the Salon jury with this work, but it was rejected. By suggesting that his nude is the queen of the hunt, he gave her just enough classical significance to make her "respectable." He admitted as much: "I intended to do nothing more than a study of the nude. But the picture was considered pretty improper, so I put a bow in the model's hand and a deer at her feet. I added the skin of an animal to make her nakedness seem less blatant. And the picture became a Diana!" Academicians had employed similar devices to give their works a moral tone or the aura of antiquity. Renoir was willing to submit to this mild form of hypocrisy, but to no avail: to the Salon jury the painting seemed harsh, coarse, and "modern."

Renoir's conception cancels out any hint of academic flavor brought by the theme. His treatment suggests that of Courbet, the "realist" and arch rebel against the academicians. The fullness of the pigment, the realization of textures, even the type of figure have a force and presence not found in Renoir's later nudes. The sand at Diana's feet does indeed look much like sand as Courbet would have represented it, but the flesh tone lacks his warmth and translucency. It is as if Renoir had subjected the figure to a bright flash of light, reducing it to almost silhouette form. Perhaps in doing this the young Renoir was influenced by Manet, for certainly this is what Manet had done in his *Déjeuner sur l'Herbe,* dated 1863.

3: LISE (1867), oil on canvas, 71½″ x 44½″
Folkwang Museum, Essen

This painting was accepted in the Salon of 1868. The Barbizon School painter Daubigny, who was sympathetic to new conceptions, was on the jury and was responsible for many members of the Impressionist group being represented at the annual exhibition which usually was open only to "official" art.

Although *Lise* owes much to Courbet, Renoir's individuality is clearly evident here. William Bürger (pseudonym for Théophile Thoré), the liberal critic, recognized this in his review of the exhibition: "The dress of white gauze, enriched at the waist by a black ribbon whose ends reach to the ground, is in full light, but with a slight greenish cast from the reflections of the foliage. The head and neck are held in a delicate half-shadow under the shade of a parasol. The effect is so natural and so true that one might very well find it false, because one is accustomed to nature represented in conventional colors. . . . Does not color depend upon the environment that surrounds it?"

Lise was an actual person. When Renoir and his painter friend Lecoeur went to Ville d'Avray not far from Paris, they would stay at the home at Lise's parents. In a sense, this painting is a portrait, for it records the likeness of a specific individual; but more accurately it can be said to be a "portrait-situation," since Renoir was not commissioned by the sitter, but, on the contrary, had used her as a model so he could paint a portrait. Manet and Degas frequently had done the same. In fact, most portraits by Impressionists are of themselves, their friends, and relatives.

4:   LA GRENOUILLÈRE (1869), oil on canvas, 26″ x 31⅞″
National Museum, Stockholm

The scene of this picture is a resort on the island of Chatou, a twenty-minute train ride from Paris and a short walk from the train station. The place was nicknamed "La Grenouillère," which means "frog pond," not because of the presence of amphibians, but rather after those ladies of easy virtue, called "grenouilles" (frogs), who frequented it. Renoir began to paint there in 1868, and the following year he was joined by Monet. They set up easels side-by-side and each painted at least three versions of the vacation spot, where city people often gathered on a pleasant summer day. The visitors are not engaging in any significant, memorable event, but they do represent *la vie moderne,* life as it is experienced by ordinary people. The event is too casual to be considered a folk ritual, but it does satisfy the dictum of the poet Baudelaire to represent the typical in contemporary life.

It is instructive to compare Monet's version (Figure 4) with that of Renoir. The light and atmosphere of this retreat on the Seine particularly attracted Monet, who makes much of the variety of reflections on the water. Renoir, similarly delighted, lacks Monet's relative single-mindedness. At this time Monet wanted to exclude all extra-visual values and capture what the eye alone could grasp, whereas Renoir's intentions were more poetic and less deliberate. He reduced value contrasts, and his brushwork is more impulsive. He fails to satisfy our curiosity with a sharp image, for his figures tend to merge with each other. Monet, on the other hand, allows forms to coalesce into spots with amazingly accurate value relationships. Renoir liked to caress the canvas, to allow his instincts as a painter to take over, and he took liberties which Monet, the stern Northerner, denied himself.

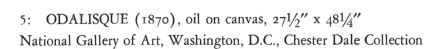

5:   ODALISQUE (1870), oil on canvas, 27½″ x 48¼″
National Gallery of Art, Washington, D.C., Chester Dale Collection

In this painting, also known as *L'Orientale* and *Woman of Algiers,* Renoir has chosen a popular romantic theme which harks back to Rubens and prefigures Matisse, and was treated by such arch rebels in art as Ingres and Delacroix. Renoir's painting can be considered as something of a tribute to Delacroix, whose art he admired greatly. He had, in fact, made a copy of Delacroix's exotic *Women of Algiers* about the same time that he painted this *Odalisque*. Later in life Renoir confided in Vollard: "One day, at the Louvre, I noticed that Rubens had obtained more by a simple rubbing than I did with all my heavy layers. Another time I discovered that Rubens produced a silver with black. I learned my lesson, of course; but does that necessarily mean I was influenced by Rubens?" Or by Delacroix, one might ask? While Renoir had heeded Delacroix in offering us "a feast to the eyes," he usually did not exploit romantic and literary subject matter. In fact, this work all but stands alone in Renoir's total *oeuvre*.

When the *Odalisque* was exhibited in the Salon of 1870, it was singled out for praise by the farsighted critic Karl Bertrand, who went so far as to say that Delacroix himself would have been willing to sign the canvas. However, Renoir's *Odalisque* is an undisguised studio work with all parts carefully selected and arranged. Vollard informs us that the model was the wife of a rug merchant. Renoir shows her as a reclining voluptuary whose monumental form all but fills the entire canvas. Her lavishly embroidered, gilded pantaloons and the gossamer delicacy of her veil and blouse so absorb the eye that her desirability as a woman is muted. Renoir has thus fused frank sensuousness with an emphatic expression of sensibility to avoid the vulgar and banal often found in such a theme.

6: SAILBOATS IN ARGENTEUIL (1873–1874), oil on canvas, 19⅞" x 25¾"
Portland Art Museum, Oregon

For a period of about three years, beginning in 1873, the Impressionists gathered at resort areas on the Seine which were easily accessible to Paris. One of these spots was Argenteuil, where Monet had a home. Caillebotte, the collector and gifted amateur painter, Sisley, Berthe Morisot, and even Manet came to Argenteuil to work. If the Impressionists ever appeared as a group with a unified purpose, it was during this period. The site offered the kind of theme they found congenial; and besides, the country was a cheaper place to live than the city, where effects of the inflationary trend that followed the war were even more keenly felt. Needless to say, the market for modern art suffered particularly at this time. "One needs considerable courage to hold on to one's brush in such times of indifference and remiss," wrote Boudin to a friend. But despite substantial reasons for despair, the works produced during this time never speak of it.

Impressionist painting of this period has been called "classical," obviously not because of the choice of subject, but because of the form and composition. There seems to be a felicitous congruence of form with intent, leading to a satisfying tranquility. The masts of the sailboats, the sails, the boats themselves, the horizon, and the reflections in the water provide horizontal and vertical rectilinear elements—areas of pattern which demand adjustment in relation to each other, to spaces between, and to the frame of the picture. Monet and Renoir tend to suppress the organic in favor of the geometric as they never have previously nor will again. Of course, they depended on their intuition and sensibility to compose, but their intent was conservative and they never radically transformed the scene before them, as would Poussin or Cézanne. Since 1869, Renoir and Monet had been painting together, often depicting identical scenes. Monet's *Sailboats* (Figure 9) is remarkably similar, but, as always, Renoir's is more richly pigmented and he introduces more activity. Contours lose some of their edge, and brushstrokes are not as consistently formed as they are in the Monet canvas. In addition, Renoir introduces curvilinear rhythms. Though both have evoked the vision of a sweet summer day, Monet appears more restrained, while Renoir seems relaxed and impulsive.

7:   LA LOGE (1874), oil on canvas, 31″ x 25″
Courtauld Institute Galleries, London

In eighteenth-century French Rococo art, love is a favored theme; men and women are frequently shown in pairs. In nineteenth-century art, with its emphasis on romantic solitude, they seem to have drifted apart. It is Renoir, with his love for the Rococo, who brings them together again. As in Rococo painting, the woman dominates as the embodiment of sensuous beauty and natural charm and grace. In this work the lady, reserved but gracious, gazes directly at the viewer. Her complexion, which is flawless and refined, is made to seem all the more so in contrast with the bearded ruddiness of her escort. Renoir proves himself to be a master of pattern in this most enchanting work. Although black was theoretically forbidden in the Impressionist palette because it is not found in nature, Renoir, nevertheless, called black "the queen of colors" and used rich blacks, not as darkening agents, but to heighten some areas, giving an almost unnatural sheen and radiance to light spaces. He avoids sharp contrasts which could jar by modulating with pale blues and grays. The model for this painting was Nina Lopez, a favorite whom Renoir described as having a profile of "antique purity." The gentleman looking through binoculars at the crowd above is the artist's younger brother Edmond.

It is interesting to note that about this time theaters were completely darkened during a performance. The gregarious Renoir disapproved of this, for he thought the theater should be well-lighted at all times. "For me, there's just as much of a show in the audience. The public is as important to me as the actors," a sentiment echoed in the attitude of the male figure in the painting.

One would never guess from this shining picture that Renoir was suffering extreme deprivation at the time it was painted. Vollard reports that the artist had nearly died of hunger and that he sold this work for only enough to pay the rent.

8:   GIRL WITH A WATERING CAN (1876), oil on canvas, 39½″ x 28¾″
National Gallery of Art, Washington, D.C., Chester Dale Collection

Renoir was obviously charmed by his little subject, as he seems to have been by children in general. This little girl, with elaborately trimmed dress and fashionable high boots, displays her "Sunday best" with evident pride. Though full of spirit, she is posed as formally as Velásquez' princesses, but unlike them, she is fully at ease in her surroundings; the freshness of the garden seems a reflection of her innocence and natural charm.

This work, which at first glance appears as artless as its subject, is subtly and exquisitely conceived. Renoir has reduced the areas of the path and the lawn to nearly flat patterns of variegated, shimmering color. His choice of color, while fundamentally naturalistic, is drawn from the "rainbow" palette of this period of pure Impressionism; tones of Prussian blue replace blacks and grays, so that blue permeates all parts of the picture and clearly implies the warm summer sky above. Renoir takes other liberties with nature, such as darkening the area directly above the head of the little girl in order to create a feeling of gentle space behind her and to call attention to the bright red ribbon nestled in her curls like another flower from the garden. The result is a magical image, in no way supernatural or bizarre, but a heightening of the beauty and grace which Renoir always found in the world around him.

9:   LE MOULIN DE LA GALETTE (1876), oil on canvas
51½″ x 69″, Louvre, Paris

In Renoir's time, that hilly section of Paris known as Montmartre still had a few windmills which had been erected when Montmartre was a small village. By the middle of the nineteenth century, Paris had grown to such an extent that Montmartre was contingent to it, and finally it was absorbed as a district within that city. By then, most of the mills had been destroyed, but Le Moulin de la Galette, the "Cake Mill," had been spared and converted into an open-air café.

While Renoir was working on this large canvas, he and his friend Georges Rivière would lug it to the site, set it up, and Renoir would engage certain of his friends to pose for him, such as the painters Frank Lamy and Solares y Cardenas, their lady friends, and models hired by Renoir. It would have been easier for Renoir to have worked from sketches in the studio, but it was important to him to capture the exact light and the precise atmospheric quality. He had, in fact, made a rapid sketch in oils in preparation for this work, probably in order to visualize the sense of the whole. After he had completed the painting, he made another, much smaller version.

The painting has acquired a predominantly blue tonality that it did not originally possess. Late in life, Renoir admitted that certain of his colors were transient and had disappeared. The blues are permanent and thus they predominate, giving the work a certain unreality which Renoir may not have intended. But it is not the color alone which determines the character of this work. Forms are diffused and contours softened. The dappling of the sunlight through the trees and the random spotting of light areas throughout the work contribute to the appearance of a shimmering vision, rich with diversions and innocent joy. The light enhances and beautifies; it destroys all blemishes.

As in the paintings by Watteau, the women occupy the central position. They make light conversation with their escorts, dance, and stroll about to visit with friends. Everyone is relaxed, receptive, and gracious.

This seemingly spontaneous painting is as complex in its composition as any Renoir ever painted. It was exhibited in the Salon of 1877, later donated to the State by the collector Caillebotte, and transferred in 1929 from the Musée Luxembourg to the Louvre.

10: MADAME CHARPENTIER AND HER CHILDREN (1878)
oil on canvas, 60½" x 74⅞"
Metropolitan Museum of Art, New York, Wolfe Fund, 1907

Renoir met the Charpentiers about 1875 through his friend Berthe Morisot, the one woman in the Impressionist group. That same year Georges Charpentier, a leading publisher, purchased Renoir's *Fisherman on a Riverbank.* His weekly review, *La Vie Moderne,* had occasionally championed new forms in art, and his interest in painting had even led him to open an art gallery. His wife, a leader in French society, held a salon at their house on the Rue de Grenelle that was frequented by the literary world, by artists, actors, politicians, and intellectuals: Zola and Alphonse Daudet, whose works Charpentier published, Hugo, Flaubert, the de Goncourt brothers, Gambetta, Clemenceau, Huysmans, Manet, Degas, Henner, and others. It was quite a plum for Renoir when Madame Charpentier chose him to paint this large-scale group portrait. In preparation for the work, Renoir made a study of his patroness, showing only her head and shoulders (Louvre, Paris). This group portrait was exhibited during the 1879 Salon and received considerable acclaim. Its success, no doubt partly due to the prestige of the subject, led to other portrait commissions for Renoir.

About this work Renoir commented: "Madame Charpentier reminded me of my early loves, the women Fragonard painted. The little girls had charming dimples in their cheeks. The family complimented me on my work. I was able to forget the journalists' abuse. I had not only free models, but obliging ones." He shows the three, accompanied by an amiable dog, in the intimacy of their elegant home with its Japanese screens; they appear as civilized, well-bred, tastefully dressed, beautiful people. Renoir departed from the easy manner of Impressionist compositions to construct this work on a pyramid. Forms have a greater solidity, although, on close examination, one can see that Renoir has built them with glazes and light impasto in a way which defies analysis. He has wedded a rather stately formal construction with a free, sensitive use of paint. The heavy use of black, not as a darkening agent but as a color, serves as a rich contrast, causing other areas to glow and shimmer.

11: MADAME CHARPENTIER AND HER CHILDREN
(detail of still life) (1878), oil on canvas
Metropolitan Museum of Art, New York, Wolfe Fund, 1907

Renoir did very few still-life paintings or pure landscapes. More interested in people, he liked to quote Pascal: "There is only one thing that interests man, and that is man." His finest still lifes are those which appear as part of a larger context, as in *Madame Charpentier and her Children* (Slide 10) and the 1881 *Luncheon of the Boating Party* (Figure 6). These still lifes do more than enrich and ornament the paintings; they suggest festivity and simple delight in fine wines, ripe, succulent fruit, glittering crystal, and fresh bouquets of flowers.

The aura of the good life is insinuated by every aspect of the two pictures mentioned. Renoir's choice of objects is significant. He did not choose the apples of Cézanne—they are too coarse; nor the asparagus, oysters, and lemons of Manet—such food is gourmet fare and somewhat too aristocratic for Renoir. He preferred bunches of grapes and pears, but especially grapes, the most sensuous of fruits: they are liquid, translucent, absorb some light, and are rich in color. Among flowers he preferred the rose, and roses appear in bouquets, adorning women's hats, and tucked in their hair. The flesh tones of his nudes have the quality of rose petals, and his roses the warmth of vibrant flesh.

The picture dealer Ambroise Vollard told this story: "On leaving Renoir's studio, I stopped to look at a study of roses, lightly brushed in. 'That's an experiment I'm making in flesh tones for a nude,' Renoir said." Evidently Renoir knew what he wanted and made a concerted effort to endow his nude figures with a roseate, blemish-free purity.

12: TWO LITTLE CIRCUS GIRLS (1879), oil on canvas
51½″ x 38½″, Art Institute of Chicago

The Impressionists exploited themes of spectacle. Degas, in particular, and, later on, Toulouse-Lautrec enjoyed the theater, particularly the popular music-hall entertainments and the circus. They had found a parallel for their enthusiasms in the Japanese print, with its scenes of famous *Kabuki* plays and the portraits of favorite actors. Renoir admired the Japanese print but was never influenced by it, at least not directly. He told Vollard, "No person should appropriate what does not belong to his own race, if he does not want to make himself ridiculous." He considered himself so much within the French tradition that he could not honestly incorporate elements from other civilizations. However, he could have found precedents in French art for these theatrical themes: in Watteau's Italian players and Daumier's savage mocking of Molière and carnival trumpery.

Renoir claimed to like the circus but not the theater, which he found artificial and pretentious. In this painting he has chosen to disregard the center ring with its main attraction and to turn his full attention to two young assistants, apparently part of a juggling act. They go through their routine in a solemn, perfunctory manner, and Renoir shows them as pensive and a bit weary. He sees their beauty, but he does not sentimentalize them. Unlike the performers in Degas' paintings, they display no particular skills; their worth is found rather in their own physical endowment, in their natural simplicity.

The scene seems to glow with a warm, orange light that gives little suggestion of circus glitter. To achieve this effect, Renoir has reduced modeling to a few accents of tone. The contours, the ribbons, the spangled fringe, so turn the eye that form is suggested without actual modeling with light and shade.

This painting was exhibited in the Impressionists' first New York show in 1886. The two young performers have been identified, from a letter in the archives of the Art Institute of Chicago, as Francesca and Angelina Wartenberg, who also performed at the celebrated Cirque Fernando.

13: THE ROWERS' LUNCH (1879–1880), oil on canvas
21½" x 25¾", Art Institute of Chicago

The two men, dressed in casual wear, appear relaxed in the presence of the young lady, whose attention is turned toward them and away from the viewer. One can assume that they, like the figures in the boats seen through the trellis archway, have been rowing and are now enjoying some relief from the exercise and heat. In all probability, the scene is the inn of Mère Fournaise on the island of Croissy and near the bridge of Chatou, where Renoir and his friends liked to lunch.

The man who smokes and leans back in his chair has been identified as Gustave Caillebotte, the wealthy engineer whose large collection of Impressionist art was bequeathed to the State when he died in 1893. At the time it was offered, there was considerable opposition from ultra-conservative elements, who maintained a violent distaste for Impressionist works. Renoir, who was executor of the estate, eventually compromised with the terms of the will and induced the State to accept a portion of this magnificent gift, which was not properly appreciated until relatively recent times.

The other man in the painting may be Victor Chocquet, the customs official who was among the first to appreciate the value of Impressionist art and to collect as much as his limited income permitted. The woman has not been identified positively, but Aline Charigot, who was to be Renoir's wife, posed for him for the *Luncheon of the Boating Party,* dated 1881 (Figure 6), and Mlle. Charigot may well be the young lady in this painting also. Although the two works are similar, the painting in the Phillips Collection is richer in content and more complex. Nevertheless, both works appear as opulent as a Veronese painting, despite the unassuming character of the company and the modesty of their intentions.

14:   SAN MARCO (1881) oil on canvas 25¾" x 32", Minneapolis Institute of Arts

This glittering tribute to the City of Canals dates from Renoir's honeymoon trip to Italy. Just before he left Paris he had discussed the beauties of Venice with Whistler, who had spent some time there and was enthusiastic about it. Renoir stopped there in the fall on his way to Rome. The character of the paintings he executed at this time suggests his delight with a city which, more than any other, is light, reflection, insubstantiality, and color. Monet, customarily a taciturn figure, was ecstatic about Venice. "All this unusual light!" he exclaimed, "It is so beautiful! I am spending wonderful moments here and can almost forget I am as old as I am." Monet was sixty-seven at the time.

In a letter to Madame Charpentier from Venice, Renoir wrote that he had discovered Tiepolo; that one can see Veronese better in Venice, but that the Louvre offered more; and that while San Marco was splendid and the Doge's Palace more splendid still, he preferred St. Germain l'Auxerrois and the sights of Paris. Even so, Renoir represents San Marco as a magnificent Byzantine gem glistening in a golden sun. His use of light glorifies the already glorious. All of Venice is there, even the tourists feeding the pigeons.

It is difficult to imagine that this painting, so full of delight and wonder, could be designated as "degenerate" by Hitler's government, which sold it to an American collector.

15:   THE BATHERS (1884-1887), oil on canvas, 45½" x 67"
Philadelphia Museum of Art, Mr. and Mrs. Carroll S. Tyson Collection

This painting belongs to that phase in Renoir's development often designated his "harsh" or "dry" period. It was the result of a temporary change of heart, for Renoir had come to believe that Impressionism, by stressing light effects at the expense of other values, led nowhere. He felt that other values, essentially traditional in nature, had been bypassed or sacrificed; he now wanted to stress drawing and the definition of contour and form and to devise compositions which were more rigorous in construction without a loss in amplitude or breadth. He had seen the frescoes of Raphael in 1882 when he visited Rome and claimed to have been inspired by them. Whether he actually was is not evident in his art of this period, which is essentially French and characteristic of Renoir. His *Bathers* recalls the bas-relief from the *Fountain of Diana* (Figure 10) in the gardens attached to the palace at Versailles. In fact, the composition of this seventeenth-century work by François Girardon was appropriated by Renoir, who reconstructed it by removing some figures and adapting others to form a pyramidal composition. The setting, however, remains truly impressionistic, and the light is so completely absorbed as part of the scene that shadow almost does not exist. There is certainly none of Courbet's bulk, nor any suggestion of naturalistic textures. Skin is opalescent, and water pearly soft. Even the rocks along the shore give an illusion of being gentle to the touch. Despite the new "discipline," the work lacks nothing in the way of innocence, bloom, and appeal.

Renoir worked on this picture for three years and then exhibited it at a commercial gallery. It was generally well-received by the public and artists alike, although Pissarro and the art critics Astruc and Huysmans voiced disapproval. Vincent van Gogh, however, admired Renoir's "pure, clean line." Renoir was pleased with the reception of his *Bathers* and concluded that he had "advanced a step in public approval."

16:   THE WASHERWOMEN (1886-1889), oil on canvas, 22¼″ x 18½″
Baltimore Museum of Art, Cone Collection

Renoir's firm belief in a patriarchal society, often quite eloqently expressed, is reflected in this painting and in others with similar themes. He never questioned the unwritten law that washing is women's work; indeed, because of this, he considered the arduous chore wholesome and natural, and his washerwomen blossom with health and contentment. To Renoir, these women are doing more than performing a service; by accepting their traditional feminine role in society they are helping to provide a stabilizing force essential to the continuing welfare of the home and humanity.

Despite its subject the painting is closer in its romantic spirit to Watteau's *Embarkation from Cythera* or Corot's *Recollection of Montfortaine* than to the toiling laundresses, often degraded by work, portrayed by Daumier, Degas, and Toulouse-Lautrec. The *Washerwomen* represents a slight turn away from the classicism of the earlier *Bathers*. Instead of the latter's relatively precise forms and recollection of French seventeenth-century classicism, the *Washerwomen* reverts to a more typical form of Renoir impressionism. Contours are softened and forms are allowed to merge with one another so that the scene seems an idyllic recollection of a distant but pleasant moment.

17:   AT THE PIANO (1892), oil on canvas
45⅝″ x 35½″, Louvre, Paris

Throughout his life, Renoir pursued themes found in Rococo art, which he loved and with which he identified. Just as Watteau, more than a century earlier, had celebrated love and music in several of his paintings, Renoir favored similar situations at this time and later, doing several paintings of a model with a mandolin. In this painting, also known as *The Daughters of Catulle Mendès,* he shows one young lady with a violin and another about to accompany her at the piano; Renoir takes a traditional subject and brings it up-to-date, giving it his own special bias. He shows non-professionals in an intimate setting, making music for personal pleasure.

Renoir enjoyed music. He had a fine, light baritone voice as a young man, and attracted the attention of a young church-choir director, Charles Gounod, later famous as the composer of the opera *Faust*. Much later, in 1882, Renoir painted a portrait of Wagner when the two were in Palermo. It is little more than a sketch, however, for the composer gave Renoir no more than a half-hour's time for a sitting, as he was in the midst of writing *Parsifal* and resented any intrusion. When quite an old man and confined to a wheelchair, Renoir was taken to the Russian Ballet, then the sensation of Paris, and delighted in the experience, which many half his age found extreme. But then Renoir was generally quite receptive to new ideas; he even expressed sympathy with the aims of abstract painting and knew of the art and ideas of Kandinsky.

18:   BATHER DRYING HER ARM (1912), oil on canvas
93″ x 74″, Museu de Arte, São Paulo, Brazil

By the time he was seventeen, Renoir had all but formed his tastes in art. "The first painters I got to know were Watteau, Lancret, and Boucher, whose *Diana at the Bath* [Figure 1] was my first great love," Renoir recalled later in life. "All my life it has held a privileged place in my heart." Renoir's tribute to the eighteenth-century master was more than a matter of words. Nearly half a century after discovering the Boucher work, he painted a somewhat similar nude, but with the pose reversed. But, while Boucher's nudes are playful and quite frankly objects for sexual pleasure, Renoir venerated women. He makes them desirable, it is true; but he also believed them to be naturally wise, practical, sensible, and good, and thought that they had qualities which a man could not acquire even though he was well aware of their existence. He also considered it a violation of nature to educate a woman as one would a man, and a terrible waste at that. "I like women best when they don't know how to read; and when they wipe their baby's behind themselves," he told his son Jean. His only comment when he heard that a certain woman had earned a degree in law was, sadly, "I cannot see myself getting in bed with a lawyer."

Renoir once told Vollard, "A painter who has the feel of breasts and buttocks is saved." One would imagine from this statement alone that Renoir's nudes would be provocative and erotic. A work such as the one in São Paulo counters this impression, as does every other Renoir nude. They are sensual, warm, frequently monumental, and alive, but there is not the slightest hint of the pornographic. They tend to assume a pose which is traditional and suggests the studio rather than the bedroom. He liked models with "skin that takes the light." It is not enough, he maintained, that a painter be an able craftsman, he must love to "caress" the canvas.

19: ON THE TERRACE (1881), oil on canvas
39⅜" x 31½", Art Institute of Chicago

Renoir used his friends and relatives as models and also engaged professionals. Later in life, he relied heavily on the girls who performed household chores for the family, recruiting them to pose. When he painted a portrait he felt obliged to capture a likeness. With models, however, especially female ones, he felt no such need. He had a concept of the ideal woman and selected models to satisfy it as closely as possible, but where nature failed he made the necessary alterations to acquire the effect he wanted. Surprisingly enough, Renoir had rather fixed notions about the matter of proportion. He thought that, ideally, the eyes should be halfway between the top of the head and the tip of the chin. If the upper half of the head dominated, he surmised, the person had an enlarged brain and was therefore an intellectual. For a woman, however, there was no worse fate! Renoir considered literary women, the "blue stockings," grossly unnatural. A low brow, on the other hand, suggested good, honest stupidity—provided it were not too low, which would indicate a stubborn nature. He liked women with small noses and small, regular teeth, with blonde or fair hair, with a flawless complexion and skin which absorbed the light. "Pouting lips," he told his son Jean, "indicate affection; thin lips, suspicion."

The woman and child in this picture appear almost suspended in a hazy, lush atmosphere which is so diffused and indefinite as to make the figures seem quite substantial by comparison. The lady, as befits her good manners, glances to one side, while the child, innocent of such niceties, fixes her gaze directly on the viewer.

20:   THE JUDGMENT OF PARIS (c. 1914), oil on canvas, 38″ x 46″
Collection of Henry P. McIlhenny, Philadelphia

The legend Renoir selected for this painting comes from Greek mythology and portrays an event which led ultimately to the Trojan War. The young shepherd Paris, the figure in the lower left of the painting, is awarding a golden apple to Venus, having chosen her the winner in this first beauty contest, begun when Eris (or Strife) had tossed the golden apple, labeled "To the Fairest," into the midst of Venus and her two competitors, Juno and Minerva. As his reward from Venus, Paris received the wife of Menelaus, Helen of Troy, considered the most beautiful woman alive. But Paris also earned the wrath of the spurned goddesses, of Helen's husband, and of all Troy.

Renoir used this theme as an opportunity to show three nudes. The goddesses are so similar as to suggest one model in three different poses. Mercury, descending upon the scene to signal the end of the contest, and Paris, too, look more like Renoir's women than men. In fact, Gabrielle, the family maid, dressed in a shepherd's habit and donned a Phrygian cap to pose for the two male characters, and Renoir did little to disguise her appearance. The effect is at once amusing and disarming, and could be considered naive except that such treatment is characteristic of the modern artist's almost total indifference to narrating a story.

The nudes, heavy-set and with a fullness in the hips that is stressed further by the smallness of the breasts, which are high and far apart, are typical of Renoir's late period. Their skin glows with an earthy ruddiness and has the firmness of adolescence. None of the figures, not even Minerva, the goddess of wisdom, seems intellectually inclined. Space is shallow; the figures dominate and fill the foreground. In this respect the painting resembles a classical bas-relief; however, the work is more in the tradition of the French sculptor Jean Goujon, whose mid-sixteenth-century *Fountain of the Innocents* Renoir knew and loved as a young man.